THE UNGRATEFUL FRIENDS

(We find ourselves encircled by individuals who lack gratitude)

Written By:

Prince Ewemade Konkons

©

Dynasty Prince Books

A publication by Dynasty Prince Books.

ISBN: 9798325666759

Printed and published in Nigeria by:

Dynasty Prince Books Publisher

Benin City

Edo State, Nigeria

Tel: +2348026233860

Copyright © 2024 Dynasty Prince Books Publishers

ISBN: 9798325666759

Lord Watch Over Your Children.

DEDICATION

To those benevolent individuals who consistently go above and beyond to assist others, even when it is inconvenient to do so, you truly embody the concept of the destined helper described in the Bible. Humanity will forever remain true to their inherent nature and purpose, and for those who possess the compassionate spirit of aiding others without expecting anything in return, you are truly deserving of admiration. Even if your efforts go unnoticed, rest assured that God acknowledges and appreciates all the benevolent acts you have performed and continue to perform in service to mankind. There is always someone out there praying for those who exemplify kindness towards others. This book is dedicated to you.

CONTENTS

BOUT THE BOOK

The literary work entitled "The Ungrateful Friends" delves into the lives of various individuals encountered from childhood to adulthood, encompassing friends, family members, schoolmates, acquaintances, colleagues, and romantic partners over the course of decades. While their true identities remain undisclosed, pseudonyms assigned by the author are utilized. The book offers an authentic portrayal of events spanning multiple decades.

Within the narrative, two prominent figures, Edingo and Astino, are emphasized, with their actions and behaviours eliciting amusement and captivation in readers. By recounting their stories, the author seeks to impart valuable lessons to younger generations of Nigerians and Africans, drawing from genuine life experiences.

A diverse ensemble of characters including Usi, Dan, Lukewell, Amino, Dond, Jumo, Fait, and others are intricately woven into the narrative, each playing a pivotal role that unfolds as readers delve further into the text.

CHAPTER ONE

INTRODUCTION ABOUT THE AUTHOR

Prince Ewemade Konkons, a committed adherent of Christianity, is a divorced father of six remarkable children, comprising four boys and two adult girls. Holding the esteemed position of Public Relations Officer for the Global Coalition for Security and Democracy in Nigeria (GCSDN), he also assumes the role of Executive Director for Avossia and Nosakhare Nig Ltd. Additionally, he is the founder of dynastyprincebooks.com and serves as the President and founder of the Aimien and Abina Foundation (A&A).

Prince Ewemade Konkons is a multifaceted individual, embodying various roles such as a comrade, writer, human rights activist, critical thinker, and advocate for the people. Driven by a revolutionary mindset, he endeavours to make a constructive impact on society.

Commencing his professional journey in the United States as a specialized security personnel, Prince Ewemade Konkons obtained an Associate of Applied Science (AAS) in Computer Information Technology from the esteemed Community College of Southern Nevada. He further pursued a Level 6 Health and Social Care Management qualification, equivalent to a BSc, from the renowned London School of

Economics. Currently, he is pursuing LLB in Law at the National Open University in London. Additionally, he has acquired a Level 7 Strategic Management and Leadership Diploma, along with various other diplomas. He was coffered with Honorary Doctorate Degree in Human Management Resource on December 12th, 2023, by The Rescue Mission Theological University in Nigeria. in Beyond his fervent passion for writing, Prince Ewemade Konkons delves into unexplored narratives, historical accounts, and significant events. His ultimate aspiration is to pave the way for future generations of Nigerians and Africans through his literary works.

Ewemade's early education in nursery and primary school was marked by success. He attended the prestigious RDC Nursery school in the upscale Government Reservation Area of Benin City, followed by enrolment at Emotan Primary School in the same city. His high school education took place at the renowned Edo College in Benin. Furthermore, Prince Ewemade Konkons actively encourages Africans to embrace and share their own narratives in their own authentic voices.

Hailing from Benin City in Edo State, Nigeria, Prince Ewemade Konkons is the first in his family to embark on a career in book writing. He began this journey after

his 50th birthday, with his book titled "The Sojourn of
an African Child." Since then, he has released numerous
other publications, including "The Refugee Project," which
coincided with World Refugee Day on June 20, 2022. Other
notable works include "Migrants Under Siege," "The
Ungrateful Friends," "Crime and Criminality Expose,"
"Trapped between two Nations," "The Secret," "Broken
Genealogy," "A Step-by-Step Approach to Legal Emigration
from Africa", "My Ghost Will Haunt You", Identifying the
Qualities of an Admirable Woman", and more.
Born on January 19, 1972, in what was formerly known as
Bendel, now Edo State, Nigeria, Prince Ewemade Konkons
grew up in a close-knit community where everyone knew
each other. Despite humble beginnings, he managed to
complete his primary and secondary education in Nigeria.
However, life took a different turn when he turned
seventeen, and he ventured into the uncertain world beyond
his home country. Prince Ewemade Konkons has been
fortunate to travel to over 50 plus countries, broadening his
perspectives and experiences.

CHAPTER TWO
THE TRAITS OF UNGRATEFUL

Definitions of an ungrateful person include an individual who demonstrates a lack of gratitude, also known as an ingrate or thankless wretch. This individual may be considered persona non grata, an unwelcome person who is not desired or accepted for some reason. It is a common aspect of human nature to experience moments of ungratefulness. In our daily lives, we may become preoccupied with our own concerns and overlook the contributions and sacrifices made by others on our behalf. Reflecting on recent events, one may likely recall instances of ingratitude. While occasional lapses in gratitude are normal, habitual ungratefulness is a distinct characteristic. Various factors, such as upbringing or past experiences, can contribute to a person's tendency towards ungrateful behavior.

However, there are individuals with certain personality traits that predispose them to higher expectations from others and the world. These individuals may struggle to comprehend the necessity of expressing gratitude for positive occurrences or the actions of others. Distinguishing between a temporary rough patch and genuine ingratitude in such individuals can prove challenging. Moreover, navigating relationships with such individuals can be exasperating and require careful consideration. The following provides a rudimentary framework for recognizing and managing ungrateful acquaintances to mitigate their adverse impact on oneself and those in their vicinity.

During my youth, I was inclined to share my possessions, offer my time and assistance, and provide shelter or financial support to those in need. However, I often found that such gestures were not reciprocated, leading me to realize the self-serving nature of many friends. Now at the age of 52, I have adopted a more cautious approach towards extending favors to others, having experienced ingratitude and exploitation firsthand. Despite having been a source of positivity and support for numerous friends and family members over the past decades, I have seldom received similar treatment in return.

The character of this book revolves around acquaintances from my childhood and encounters made during my life's journey. Astino, a childhood friend, and I both grew up in the same community. We shared a close bond with other friends, engaging in various activities together. At the age of 18, I rented my first room from Astino's father, solidifying the close relationship between our families. Astino, along with another close friend named Ehgisi, played a significant role in planning my first journey outside of Africa. Despite Ehgisi's arrogant demeanor, which often distanced me from him, Astino maintained a strong friendship with him. My perception of Astino evolved over time, as I accepted individuals based on their presented selves without prejudice. Astino became like a brother and a dear friend to me.

Unbeknownst to me, Asino was not the person I believed him to be. He exhibited a tendency to assert dominance and superiority over others, viewing himself as a demigod who sought to dictate the fate of those around him and claim credit for their achievements. Asino displayed a humorous demeanor, yet harbored feelings of envy and jealousy towards his close associates, desiring to exert control over their lives as well.

(Indicators of ungrateful companions.)

PEOPLE NEVER REMEMBER THE MILLION TIMES YOU'VE HELPED THEM, ONLY THE ONE TIME YOU DON'T.

CHAPTER THREE
WHO ARE THE UNGRATEFUL?

Individuals who exhibit ingratitude often display traits such as an inflated sense of self-importance, arrogance, vanity, and a constant need for admiration and validation. These ungrateful individuals frequently demonstrate selfish behavior and may exploit your kindness by repeatedly requesting favors or treating you as a personal resource, expecting unwavering support. Moreover, they typically fail to acknowledge or express gratitude for your efforts and seldom reciprocate any acts of kindness. This lack of appreciation is a common concern among parents and children alike, reflecting a pervasive issue that many can relate to. Whether it be a spouse, a superior at work, or a friend, encountering ingratitude can be challenging. How does one navigate relationships with those who demonstrate ingratitude, especially after extending significant efforts on their behalf? While this may not be a simple task, it is important to approach such situations with a mindset of altruism, understanding that not everyone will recognize or value your sacrifices. Despite any feelings of disappointment or frustration, it is crucial to maintain a sense of generosity without expecting reciprocation, recognizing that not everyone possesses the same level of gratitude or empathy. Accepting the reality of ingratitude, even from close relations, can be a difficult process that requires time and introspection.

It is often said that individuals who aid should possess a short memory, while those who receive aid should cultivate a long memory. The actions of helping, giving, and facilitating are closely linked with expressions of gratitude. Assisting others undoubtedly brings a sense of personal fulfillment. Equally important, however, is the acknowledgment and appreciation received in return for one's efforts, attention, or time. The absence of gratitude can leave one feeling depleted, even when the act of helping is inherently rewarding. Some individuals, however, fail to adopt this perspective. These individuals may be deemed ungrateful, as they fail to recognize or value the assistance provided to them. Not only do they disregard the help they receive, but they may also continue to make demands for further favors, establishing a pattern of entitlement. Should one choose to discontinue their assistance, suspecting manipulation or exploitation, they may be met with accusations of lacking empathy, inducing feelings of guilt. What motivates the behavior of ungrateful individuals remains a subject of inquiry. Traditionally, gratitude was understood as a sentiment evoked by acts of kindness or generosity directed towards oneself. Whether in the form of a helping hand, a thoughtful gift, or the investment of time, these gestures were believed to trigger feelings of gratitude.

However, gratitude encompasses more than just an emotional response; it also includes a cognitive aspect. To experience gratitude, individuals must first possess the ability to appreciate. This involves recognizing the kind gestures made towards them, acknowledging the positive impact of those gestures, and understanding the effort or intention behind them. The capacity for appreciation is a skill that ungrateful individuals often lack.

Psychologists at Hope College in Michigan assert that ungrateful individuals are deficient in their ability to feel grateful. They argue that gratitude is characterized by a sense of abundance, coupled with an awareness of being the recipient of a valuable gift from a giver. This necessitates a genuine appreciation for the act itself. Furthermore, they emphasize that gratitude involves a complex interplay between donors, gifts, recipients, and the attitudes of all parties involved, making it a deeply social emotion.

Researchers at the University of Manchester take this concept a step further by suggesting that gratitude is not only a skill but also a dispositional trait. They propose that gratitude is an overarching attitude towards life that involves recognizing and valuing the positive aspects of the world. Consequently, individuals who struggle to feel grateful may be predisposed to view favours, assistance, or gifts as inadequate or unworthy, thereby hindering their ability to experience gratitude.

This suggests that ingratitude may manifest early in life.

The failure of parents to instill a sense of appreciation in their children may lead to the development of Emperor Syndrome. Consequently, individuals may carry this egocentric perspective into adulthood, expecting others to fulfill their needs and desires. Such a worldview impedes the ability to feel gratitude.

The 5 risks faced by individuals who exhibit ingratitude: Ingratitude is a detrimental trait that can lead to various negative consequences. Those who fail to express gratitude towards others may find themselves facing the following risks:

1. Chronic unhappiness: According to Mokokoma Mokhonoana, unhappiness is a result of a chronic lack of gratitude. Scientific research supports this claim, showing that the ability to experience gratitude is closely linked to higher levels of happiness. A study conducted at Hope College in Michigan further demonstrated that gratitude serves as a strong predictor of overall happiness, well-being, and life satisfaction. In contrast, individuals who are ungrateful may find themselves trapped in a cycle of chronic unhappiness. Without the ability to appreciate the help of others or the beauty of life itself, they are more likely to experience perpetual dissatisfaction.
2. Being tied to trauma, gratitude serves as a valuable tool in managing adverse situations and

psychological traumas. Various studies have demonstrated that individuals can experience feelings of gratitude even amidst challenging circumstances. Those who exhibit a quicker recovery from trauma are often those who cultivate a focus on the positive aspects of their lives, expressing gratitude for them rather than dwelling on losses or deficiencies.

3. The practice of reassessing situations from a benefits-oriented perspective fosters a more positive outlook, triggering beneficial emotions and eliciting positive neurophysiological responses. Gratitude aids in disengaging from toxic emotions and repetitive negative thoughts, enabling individuals to concentrate on the positive aspects of their lives. As Sonja Lyubomirsky aptly stated, "Gratitude serves as a remedy for

negative emotions, countering feelings of envy, hostility, worry, and irritation."

4. Moreover, a lack of gratitude can lead to an unhealthy psychological state characterized by cycles of unrealistic expectations and frustrations, hindering one's ability to fully appreciate positive experiences. Consequently, a study conducted at Virginia Commonwealth University has revealed that ungrateful individuals face an increased risk of

developing mental disorders such as major depression, generalized anxiety disorder, various phobias, bulimia nervosa, and engaging in addictive behaviours involving nicotine, alcohol, and drugs.

One of the greatest perils faced by ungrateful individuals is being condemned to despair. Ungratefulness can lead to a self-fulfilling prophecy, as it causes others to cease their acts of kindness towards them. Consequently, ungrateful individuals find themselves ensnared in the very trap they have constructed. Deprived of assistance, they may perceive the world as a hostile environment devoid of benevolence, failing to recognize that their own attitudes have alienated them from others, resulting in their isolation.

Research conducted at the University of Manchester has revealed that ungrateful individuals exhibit a greater dependence and diminished autonomy compared to those who cultivate gratitude, indicating a profound need for interpersonal connections. Furthermore, such individuals often struggle with self-acceptance and lack a sense of purpose in life.

5.Moreover, ungratefulness not only fosters bitterness but can also have adverse effects on physical health. Studies have demonstrated that gratitude can reduce levels of stress, anxiety, and worry. Consequently, it is unsurprising that research at the University of Michigan has shown ungrateful individuals to frequently report heightened stress levels and a greater prevalence of physical symptoms.

Gratitude significantly enhances the quality of sleep, facilitating faster and more restful slumber. This is attributed to its ability to counteract negative thoughts that often hinder the onset of sleep. Fortunately, gratitude is a trait that can be cultivated. An individual need not remain mired in ungratefulness indefinitely; the key lies in refraining from taking blessings for granted and viewing life as a precious gift. As Thornton Wilder, the esteemed novelist, aptly noted, "We can only say that we are alive in those moments when our hearts are aware of our treasures.

(Individuals who demonstrate ingratitude.)

CHAPTER FOUR
THE STORY OF EDINGO

The individual whose story is detailed in this chapter of the book is not actually named Edingo, as the narrator has chosen to refer to them as such. It is important to note that Edingo and the narrator did not have a preexisting friendship or acquaintance from childhood. Their relationship began in the summer of 2005, facilitated by a mutual acquaintance named Jumo, who was a close friend of the narrator and regarded as a younger sister. Edingo, a Nigerian by birth with Dutch citizenship, was visiting Nigeria at the time. Hailing from a wealthy family in Benin City, Edo State, Nigeria, he was the eldest son of a prominent figure in Nigerian society. Edingo and Jumo were romantically involved, and through Jumo's introduction, the narrator and Edingo developed a close friendship. Edingo was facing significant challenges in his relationship with his father, leading to a strained dynamic between them. This strained relationship often resulted in Edingo spending minimal time in Nigeria before returning to his work in a factory in the Netherlands. Jumo, a knowledgeable and spiritually connected individual, was well-known in the city and played a pivotal role in bringing Edingo and the narrator together.

Jumo played a significant role in Edingo's life, as he endeavored to establish a hotel business in the city center. With Jumo's assistance, Edingo successfully sold some of his family's property to initiate the hotel construction project. Jumo, being a highly intelligent individual, proposed the idea of incorporating a drinking bar within the hotel premises, which resulted in a flourishing business. However, complications arose when Jumo became pregnant before the year ended and expressed her desire to travel abroad for childbirth. Despite her wishes, Edingo insisted that she remain in Nigeria to focus on the ongoing project while he was away in The Netherlands. Upon the narrator's return from Europe in the summer of 2007, Jumo personally greeted him at the airport in Lagos and accompanied him on the journey to Benin City. Subsequently, Jumo visited the narrator at his residence in the Government Reservation Area of Benin, where she disclosed her urgent need to travel abroad for childbirth in September 2007. She emphasized the importance of the narrator's support for her well-being and safety during this crucial time.

The narrator pondered these thoughts throughout the night and subsequently contacted Jumo to inquire about the possession of a passport. Jumo confirmed that she did indeed possess a passport. Following this confirmation, the narrator completed all necessary procedures and submitted both Jumo's and their own passports at the Ireland Embassy in Abuja. Jumo underwent an interview and was instructed to return in seven days to collect the issued visa. Jumo then purchased a ticket and traveled from Nigeria to Dublin, where she was greeted by an old classmate of the narrator. Meanwhile, the narrator arrived from Milan, Italy, after visiting an old friend. As Jumo's due date approached, it became evident that she lacked the requisite legal documentation to remain in Ireland. Consequently, her only viable option was to apply for asylum, allowing her to give birth at the government's expense. Despite her due date passing, Jumo faced complications during labor due to her placenta obstructing the birth canal. Despite medical recommendations for a cesarean section, Jumo adamantly refused, citing her faith and belief in a natural birth. After days of persuasion from the narrator, Jumo eventually consented to the procedure. The operation was successful, and Jumo gave birth to a baby boy.

In the subsequent year, the Narrator revisited Nigeria for his customary welding in December 2008. Following the completion of his welding duties in Nigeria, he embarked on his journey back to Dublin, Ireland. However, he encountered a setback when he was denied entry and subsequently returned to Nigeria. Meanwhile, Jumo boy Edingo was also in Nigeria, endeavoring to advance his hotel construction project by liquidating certain family assets, including a property that had been on the market for several months. Despite his efforts, Edingo faced numerous obstacles, ranging from familial disputes to logistical challenges. Seeking assistance, Edingo approached the Narrator and detailed the prolonged struggle to sell the property, valued at One hundred and fifty million Naira (150,000,000). He expressed his desire for the Narrator's help in selling the property and mentioned plans to provide financial compensation to facilitate the launch of an importation business from China.

The Narrator took the initiative to arrange a meeting with all relevant parties, including Edingo's younger brother's close friends and the Narrator's family relatives who held significant influence in the city. The meeting took place at the Motor Park in the city. During the meeting, Edingo pledged to gift two brand new Kia vehicles to the Narrator's cousins, who had resolved a dispute that had hindered the sale of a property. Following the meeting, the Narrator enlisted the help of a talisman who was closely associated with him. Edingo also promised to provide a substantial sum of money to the talisman. Subsequently, the Narrator took Edingo to his spiritual father's house for prayer. The spiritualist asked Edingo what he would do for God if the property was sold within two weeks. Edingo pledged to donate a parcel of land measuring 100X100 and a cash amount of eight hundred thousand naira for the establishment of a church. The spiritual leader requested to be taken to the property site for a cleansing prayer session. As Edingo was short of funds, the Narrator covered all expenses for the prayer session. A few days later, the Narrator received a call from Edingo's younger sister, informing him that Edingo was in distress and required immediate attention. The Narrator rushed to the hotel building site where Edingo was found in a completed unit. Edingo was taken to the same spiritualist who had previously prayed over the property. The spiritualist requested funds to purchase materials for an urgent prayer session for Edingo, which the Narrator covered with his own personal funds. Edingo recovered fully after the prayer session. During the waiting period for the property sale, the Narrator personally provided meals for Edingo, who frequently visited the Narrator's residence.

Prior to the conclusion of the second week, a prospective buyer emerged unexpectedly, expressing immediate readiness to purchase the property. The offer presented amounted to one hundred and twenty million, with ten million designated for both Edingo and his half-brother, and the remaining one hundred million to be settled in the presence of their father, who was already present. The buyers sought assurance of the transaction's authenticity, hence requested for the entire process to be documented. Ultimately, the transaction was successfully completed.

After this event, Edingo began displaying peculiar behaviour, though I maintained composure and remained unconcerned. My apprehension, however, pertained to those who had assisted him on my behalf and the commitments he had made to them. After a period of five days, Edingo offered me two hundred thousand naira, allocating fifty thousand naira for the Talisman, but neglecting to provide any compensation to the Man of God. I declined the money and advised him to personally deliver the fifty thousand naira to the Talisman. To date, he has not expressed gratitude to either party.

Following this, Edingo embarked on a two-month journey abroad, returning thereafter. Upon learning of his return, I distanced myself from him for a year. Despite his attempts to seek forgiveness through mutual acquaintances, I eventually relented and visited him at the construction site of the hotel. On that evening, he expressed great delight and appreciation for my presence, receiving a standing ovation from all esteemed individuals in attendance.

Our friendship recommended from that point onward, with a notable shift in his financial situation leading to increased property sales. Despite the completion of his hotel building, he did not extend any financial assistance to me, nor did I request any from him. This decision caused dissatisfaction among the individuals I had enlisted to aid him. I had to counsel them to relinquish control to a higher power, recognizing that all possessions ultimately belong to a higher authority and are transient. Over time, our paths diverged as his obsession with wealth intensified. Nevertheless, he continued to show me respect whenever I visited his hotel. He persistently urged me to join him in revelry and socializing with women involved in illicit activities at his establishment, a lifestyle I found unappealing. Subsequently, we drifted apart, and I traveled abroad. As the years passed, we reestablished communication, with me residing in Sweden. He expressed a desire to visit me in the autumn of 2019, which he eventually did, staying at my residence. During this period, we endeavored to rebuild our relationship. He disclosed his substantial financial holdings, derived from selling his deceased father's assets in Abuja, Nigeria, as the eldest son now overseeing his father's estate. He mentioned a property valued at over One billion Naira, which he intended to invest in Europe. I helped in securing apartment units in France through a contact in Paris specializing in real estate. However, he proposed focusing on exporting goods to Nigeria for resale. After deliberation, we settled on used computers as the venture. I advised against involving his associates in Nigeria, stating my intention to withdraw from the arrangement if they were included. He agreed to my terms, providing the funds for the business. We procured laptops, along with a C 200 Mercedes Ben wagon and a Volkswagen Sharan van, loaded the computers into the

vehicles, and shipped them to Lagos, Nigeria. The laptops were intended to be sold by my contact in Lagos, a long-standing acquaintance who has served as my business partner over the years. Upon the arrival of the goods in Lagos, he requested that the Volkswagen Sharan van be taken to his residence in Lagos, while the Mercedes was to be delivered to my business partner. However, the laptop business did not yield the expected sales, leading to his impatience and desire for his associates to take possession of the vehicle and laptops. This deviation from our initial agreement provoked my anger, as I had devoted considerable time and effort to loading the vehicle. Consequently, I decided to seize and sell the goods without remitting any funds to him, as a form of retribution for his actions towards me and my associates. Life cannot solely revolve around his desires and demands.

Several weeks later, he fell ill and was hospitalized at Malmö Hospital after suffering a stroke that nearly claimed his life. His survival following more than two weeks in the intensive care unit was deemed miraculous, as the odds seemed stacked against him. Despite the immense challenges, my children's mother and I set aside our work and familial obligations to care for him during his hospitalization. After enduring two months of stress, we managed to facilitate the arrival of his wife from Nigeria with the hospital's assistance. Following his discharge, he was transferred to the Netherlands for further medical attention. Regrettably, he has not expressed any gratitude for our efforts. It is disheartening to witness such ingratitude, prompting one to question whether it is inherent in human nature or merely a personal trait.

Edingo still owes me, and he will eventually repay his debt, if we are granted the gift of life, sound mind, and good health by the grace of God.

They exploit your assistance in ascending the ladder of success, only to discard you once their objectives have been met.

I HAVE LEARNT SILENCE FROM THE TALKATIVE,
TOLERATION FROM THE INTOLERANT, AND KINDNESS
FROM THE UNKIND; YET STRANGE, I AM UNGRATEFUL TO
THESE TEACHERS.

" DO NOT SPOIL WHAT YOU HAVE BY DESIRING WHAT YOU
HAVE NOT; REMEMBER THAT WHAT YOU NOW HAVE WAS
ONCE AMONG THE THINGS YOU ONLY HOPEED FOR."

CHAPTER FIVE

THE STORY OF ASINO

Asino, a childhood friend with whom we grew up in the same neighborhood, had two brothers and three sisters who all resided in their father's household. Over time, it was revealed that my father's immediate elder sister's third daughter was married to Asino's uncle, further strengthening our bond as families living in the same community. Subsequently, I rented a room in Asino's father's residence, solidifying our friendship. Our group of childhood friends frequently gathered at Asino's house, spending evenings chatting together most of the evenings and weekends. In the early 1993s, there was a collective desire among the youths to travel abroad. Asino eventually journeyed to Gambia and assisted other young men from our neighborhood in finding routes out of Nigeria through Benin Republic, Mali, and Senegal. Some of our friends attempted the Libyan route but ultimately returned home after facing challenges reaching European countries. Upon Asino's return without success, he began recruiting young men from our neighborhood for similar journeys. After a long discussion with Asino's on one faithful evening, myself, and another friend, Usi, who had also embarked on a similar journey, I and three other friends decided to take the leap, understanding that luck played a significant role in such endeavors.

Several weeks later, two companions and I agreed to undertake a journey. Asino was informed of our plans and requested a meeting to discuss the upcoming trip. During our conversation, he mentioned that his cousin was also interested in joining us. On October 1st, 1993, three friends and I set out on the journey. I possessed an Austrian visa, allowing me to travel through Cabo Verde, an island off the coast of Senegal. At that time, it was more convenient to travel from countries other than Nigeria, as many Nigerians were being turned away for using Balkan Airlines, the most affordable and accommodating airline of that period.

On August 14th, 1998, I made my first visit to Nigeria from the United States, after been away for five years. Upon arrival, I sought out Asino and paid a visit to his father, as well as reconnecting with old acquaintances in the area. Most of them had relocated abroad, but I was able to reunite with those who remained. Throughout my stay Lagos, Nigeria, I included Asino in my activities, sharing clothes and accommodations in a Lagos hotel. I provided support and companionship as any good friend would, before returning to the United States.

Over the course of the year, I began assisting Asino with obtaining visas for various countries to aid those in need within our community. After relocating to Belgium, some years later. I ventured into the exportation of cars to Nigeria. During this time, two Mercedes C230 Coupes that I had exported encountered issues, leading Asino to express interest in purchasing one of the cars from me. Without hesitation, I sold him the vehicle at a discounted price, as our friendship held more value to me than profit. Subsequently, he repaired and sold the car for a substantial sum, which provided him with financial stability. He later approached me for the purchase of another car, which I again sold to him at a discounted rate. As he continued to profit from these transactions, I found satisfaction in supporting my childhood friend, prioritizing camaraderie over monetary gain. Upon returning to Belgium, Asino requested a car for his father, prompting me to gift him a Volvo blue 760 that I had acquired from a dealer in Antwerp. Despite my altruistic gesture, it became apparent that my generosity went unnoticed, as Asino failed to acknowledge my contributions to his family's well-being. Despite his reluctance to acknowledge my acts of kindness, I remained steadfast in my commitment to supporting him and his loved ones. After a few years, I returned to Nigeria to settle down. Unfortunately, during this time, I encountered difficulties as Asino took advantage of my vulnerable state. He displayed a side of himself that was previously unknown to me. Whenever I left the company of friends, he would maliciously spread rumours about me, claiming that I believed I was the only one capable of achieving success abroad. Despite hearing negative remarks about Asino from others, I consistently defended him in his absence. However, my loyalty was tested when I overheard a conversation about Asino selling fraudulent properties in the community. I confronted the individuals discussing this matter and insisted that Asino be present to address the accusations. It became evident that Asino was ungrateful and deceitful, traits that I had failed to recognize in a friend.

Asino has received more benefits from me than all my childhood friends combined. Despite the assistance I have provided him, he has chosen not to acknowledge it, opting instead to speak negatively of me whenever the opportunity presents itself. He has maintained a facade of friendship while his actions reveal his true nature as an adversary. Known for his cunning ability to gather information about others while keeping his own personal details guarded, those familiar with him describe him as a deceptive individual, often likening him to a chameleon.
I now interact with Asino from a distance, following the adage that one must handle dealings with a malevolent entity with caution. This precaution serves as a safeguard against allowing him to come too close.
Asino and his family currently reside in the United States. Occasionally, his relatives remark to me that his relocation to

the United States may test his perceived wealth, as he appears to believe that money is easily obtained in that country. It is suggested that he should share his resources with others. Ultimately, all individuals will be held accountable for their actions, both positive and negative.

(This was the situation involving Asino in the capacity of a friend.)

CHAPTER SIX
THEY ARE PART OF OUR FAMILY CIRCLE

Ungrateful individuals can also be found within our own family circle. These individuals often take advantage of our generosity, as we tend to go above and beyond to fulfil their needs due to our familial connection. Unfortunately, they may betray the trust we have placed in them.

I can provide a personal example involving my immediate elder sister, whom I will refer to as Amino for the purpose of this account. Amino and I were raised together in the same household, experiencing a tumultuous relationship. After embarking on a journey in pursuit of better opportunities and adventures, I returned to Nigeria for a visit after many years away.

During my visit, Amino and my other half-sister greeted and received me in Lagos before traveling together to Benin. Upon our arrival, I presented gifts I had brought back from the United States to my family members. While distributing the gifts, I noticed Amino's eagerness to claim items intended for my half-sister, despite already receiving her own gifts. This incident served as a precursor to her ungrateful behaviour that would manifest in the future.

Personally, I overlooked her minor actions, considering our close familial bond as siblings. However, her persistent and similar behaviour towards me became apparent over the years. It became clear that her intentions were to harm me and seize my assets. This culminated in a significant conflict in May 2004, which irrevocably altered our relationship.

In hindsight, she had revealed her true intentions during my initial visit to Nigeria after years of absence. Amino repaid my kindness and support (including a monthly salary for her late husband, cars for both, and the building of her home) with malice.

Amino embodies the definition of ingratitude within a family. Her actions demonstrate the importance of caution when dealing with such individuals.

My experience with Amino has provided valuable lessons that will guide me for the rest of my life.

(They are part of the family.)

CHAPTER SEVEN
WE HAVE THEM AS FRIENDS

Ungrateful individuals are ubiquitous, surfacing in various
societal contexts: family, friendships, workplaces, religious
institutions, and everyday interactions.

This chapter focuses on an acquaintance named Dan
(fictitious for anonymity). Our paths crossed in Montreal,
Canada, during the frigid winter of 1994. Dan a Nigerian
who had arrived from the Netherlands, I was residing at the
YMCA. Prior to Dan's arrival, I had befriended Newt,
another Nigerian national. As the first Nigerian he
encountered upon his arrival, I introduced Newt to the city.
Newt and Dan shared a pre-existing friendship from the
Netherlands, and we formed a close bond in Montreal. We
rented apartments in the same building, with my residence
on the first floor, Dan's on the second, and Newt's on the
third, illustrating our proximity.

Over the ensuing years, our aspirations led us to seek
opportunities in the United States. In the fall of 1995, I
relocated to Boston, Massachusetts, leaving Dan and Newt
behind in Montreal. A year later, I moved to Richmond,
California, and two years after that, I settled in Reno,
Nevada. Six months after Newt's arrival in the United
States, he briefly resided with me while securing his own

accommodation. During this time, I was enrolled at the Community College of Southern Nevada, pursuing a degree in Information Technology.

In 1998, I relocated to Las Vegas, Nevada, to continue my education at CCSN's campus there. By this time, Newt had also established himself in Las Vegas. The following year, Dan arrived in the United States from Canada. He initially stayed with Newt but would often visit me during the day.

During that summer, I had established the first African Caribbean grocery store in the city centre. Dan frequently assisted me at the store. I facilitated introductions between my female classmates and Newt and Dan, enabling them to marry and obtain their Green Cards. Newt married a woman named Shinai, while Dan wed another acquaintance of mine. I also served as their legal counsel, assisting them with the necessary paperwork for their residency applications. These acts of assistance were performed with genuine goodwill. I extended similar support to other individuals who had relocated from Montreal, Canada, including those who were friends with Dan and Newt. I did not know many of them personally. Life seemed to be flourishing, and all appeared well. I transitioned into the role of an investor, particularly focusing on supporting individuals with whom I shared a long history, such as my business partner Dan. Our partnership spanned various ventures, from exporting goods to engaging in diverse business activities. Dan greatly benefited from our relationship, as he grew closer to me than our mutual acquaintance, Newt, who worked as a security officer at a casino and had limited time to spend with us. Despite occasional meetings at Newt's residence during lunch breaks, jealousy over my bond with Dan did not concern me. Over time, Dan and I developed such a strong connection that observers often mistook us for twins due to our similar appearance and shared preferences in clothing, footwear, and home decor.

In 2001, I faced a significant setback with the closure of my business and entrusted Dan with all my business affairs, including my bank card and pending payments for a transaction with my products suppliers. In New York. Unfortunately, Dan took advantage of my vulnerability and deceived my then girlfriend into believing that my assets were frozen by the banks. Unbeknownst to him, my business associate in New York verified the situation, leading to the discovery of Dan's deceitful actions. While I sought financial assistance from others, Dan clandestinely retained control of my funds.

During a chance encounter with Newt at Paris Charles de Gaulle Airport in 2005, he revealed his knowledge of Dan's betrayal and expressed regret over his inability to warn me sooner. Reflecting on the situation, we shared a moment of understanding before continuing our respective journeys. Subsequently, I confronted Dan about his actions and urged him to return my money before visiting Nigeria. Dan avoided the country for a period and maintained a low profile upon his return, driving a distinct green Nissan Armada SUV. Upon locating him in Benin City, I confronted him in a secluded area, questioning his motives and leaving the resolution of our conflict to a higher power.

From that day forward, I entrusted all matters concerning him to the divine providence. Nemesis, with its inexorable nature, inevitably caught up with him. By the end of 2022, I reached out to Dan to inquire about his well-being, only to discover that he had been stricken with a debilitating stroke, rendering him unable to walk or communicate effectively. My heart was heavy with sorrow and empathy for his plight. It is a testament to the righteousness of our Creator that such injustices do not go unnoticed.

CHAPTER EIGHT

THE STORY OF LUKEWLL

This is the tale of an individual whom I encountered and subsequently formed a friendship with, whom I shall refer to as Lukewell for the purpose of this narrative. Lukewell and I crossed paths in Reno, Nevada, during my tenure as a student at Truckee Meadows Community College (TMCC). In search of supplementary employment, I frequently visited various car rental stands near the airport, ultimately arriving at Dollar Rent car stand where I encountered Lukewell. He was stationed at the rental counter as a car rental assistant and upon inquiring about potential job opportunities, he promptly directed me to the manager. Thus began a burgeoning friendship between Lukewell and me.

Our bond deepened as we both relocated to Las Vegas, where I had established an African shop. Lukewell visited my shop and revealed his presence in the city. Over the years, our friendship endured until the autumn of 2001, when I found myself facing business challenges that necessitated a change in ownership to prevent confiscation by the Department of Treasury. Turning to Lukewell for assistance, I proposed selling the business to him. While initially hesitant due to financial constraints, Lukewell eventually agreed to a purchase arrangement.

After conducting an inventory, the business was valued at $102,000, with a negotiated sale price of $65,000. Lukewell made a down payment of $20,000 and committed to monthly instalments of $1,000. I included a provision that upon adherence to the payment plan for two years, I would consider forgiving a portion of the remaining balance. True to his word, Lukewell diligently fulfilled his monthly obligations. In April 2004, I decided to waive the outstanding balance as a gesture of goodwill, much to Lukewell's satisfaction. With the transfer of ownership complete, the business transitioned seamlessly under Lukewell's stewardship, marking the culmination of our shared journey.

Over the passing years, our communication has been maintained diligently. I consistently make a point to inquire about his well-being and the status of his business annually. Occasionally, I would also inquire about my previous client through him. In July of 2022, I found myself in need of his assistance. Specifically, I required a money order amounting to $930 to facilitate the filing of my application 1-601 with the Department of Homeland Security in the United States. Lukewell was the first person to come to mind for this task. I reached out to him via WhatsApp, expressing my need for his help and requesting a conversation at his earliest convenience. A day later, he returned my call and apologized for the delay. I reassured him that there was no need for an apology. I proceeded to outline the assistance I required from him. He assured me that he would follow up, but unfortunately, he never did. Furthermore, he proceeded to block me on WhatsApp and has not returned any of my subsequent calls since.

It is truly baffling how easily individuals can overlook the generosity of a man who generously invested over $25,000 in their business endeavours. The complexities of life, as they often say, run deep.

I have always maintained a sense of faith in humanity, yet my trust was shattered by Lukewell. I extended to him the opportunity to take ownership of a business that I had painstakingly nurtured over the years. The business was thriving, capable of meeting all financial obligations, sustaining a team of three employees, and even turning a profit. Situated in the bustling heart of Las Vegas, it was a venture of great promise.

There have been others who have similarly disappointed me, though I choose to focus on those whose actions have caused me the greatest sorrow. In due time, our paths will cross once more.

(Lukewell exemplifies the characteristics of an ungrateful friend)

CHAPTER NINE
WE HAVE THEM AS COLLEGUES

Things to be mindful of when working with unappreciative colleagues. Navigating interactions with ungrateful colleagues can be challenging, yet it is a common experience in the workplace. Whether it involves managing a difficult client or dealing with an unappreciative peer, maintaining composure, demonstrating kindness, and establishing boundaries are key strategies. While it may not always be possible to change the behaviour of an ungrateful colleague, one can showcase effective conflict resolution skills to others. Identify reasons for their lack of gratitude and provide an opportunity for them to respond. Avoid assigning blame and instead use statements that express your feelings. For instance, you could communicate, "I perceive a lack of acknowledgment for the support I provide on work projects, despite our differing organizational affiliations." Maintain an assertive yet open demeanour during these discussions.

The following are indicative characteristics of a toxic and ungrateful colleague:

- Demonstrating rudeness and disrespect towards others.

- Engaging in confrontational and aggressive behaviour.
- Habitually shifting blame onto others for their own mistakes.
- Displaying greed and perpetual dissatisfaction
- Exhibiting a know-it-all attitude.
- Employing sarcasm and ridicule to belittle others It is imperative to remain vigilant for ungrateful individuals, even within the workplace, as they may be present in various forms.

The definition of 'entitled' according to the Cambridge Dictionary is: "Feeling that one has the inherent right to obtain or achieve desired outcomes without exerting effort or demonstrating merit, solely based on one's identity." When entrepreneurs' express frustration about their "ungrateful and entitled employee," what precisely do they mean? Certain colleagues or team members may harbour the belief that they are inherently deserving of privileges such as flexible work arrangements, salary increases, and career advancements, irrespective of their level of dedication. Furthermore, they may exhibit dissatisfaction or ingratitude towards the support provided to them. Does this scenario resonate with you? Effectively managing an employee or colleague who consistently expects more than what is warranted can prove to be a formidable challenge. This behaviour is not only time-consuming and draining but can also have detrimental effects on the overall dynamics of the business or professional relationship. It is indeed a problematic issue. The resolution of such conflicts often hinges on the nature of the employee's grievances. If the individual insists on higher compensation or perceives an inequality in remuneration despite the company's financial constraints, the employer may find themselves in a difficult position. However, if the employee argues for remote work privileges based on their non-customer-facing role, a potential compromise may be worth considering. As a leader, your primary challenge lies in discerning whether the employee's demands are grounded or if they are simply asserting their entitlement without valid justification. Additionally, it is crucial to consider the ripple effects of your decisions on the broader team dynamics.

Recognizing the Ungrateful and Entitled

Behaviours to Spot:

- **Excessive Complaining:** Individuals focus on their own grievances, disregarding team and company well-being. They often compare themselves to others for perceived unfairness.

- **Constant Dissatisfaction:** Benefits and rewards fail to motivate these individuals. They may exhibit indifference towards promotions or pay increases.
- **Disruptive Behaviour:** They spread negativity and bad-mouth the company and leadership, creating a toxic work environment.

Self-Reflection:

Consider whether your actions or business decisions contribute to an entitlement culture. Ensure clear and consistent treatment of employees.

Solution:

Create a comprehensive employee handbook that outlines expectations for both employees and management. This document promotes fairness and clarity in employment practices.

(In the realms of our labour, we find their presence.)

CHAPTER TEN
THEY ARE PERPETAULLY DISCONTENT

Ungrateful individuals seem to be perpetually discontent, regardless of the efforts made on their behalf. Their inherent nature compels them to exploit those around them, taking their presence for granted and failing to acknowledge the blessings in their lives. They maintain an insatiable desire for more, never finding contentment in what they possess. This relentless dissatisfaction can be deeply frustrating, leaving you with feelings of inadequacy.

It is futile to strive for their happiness. Ungrateful people are consumed by self-interest, expecting others to prioritize their needs above their own. Their endless complaints and negative outlook create a toxic environment.

However, it is crucial to recognize that happiness originates within the mind. Even ungrateful, unkind, and malicious individuals can choose to experience contentment. Their thoughts determine their level of satisfaction. When thoughts lack appreciation, gratitude will be scarce.

Investing energy in the wrong places due to a failure to appreciate the good inevitably leads to further dissatisfaction. The desperate pursuit of happiness in external possessions will not yield true gratitude. It is akin to chasing mirages, never achieving anything substantial to be grateful for.

Let us cultivate gratitude for the small acts of kindness we receive, avoiding the trap of taking things for granted.

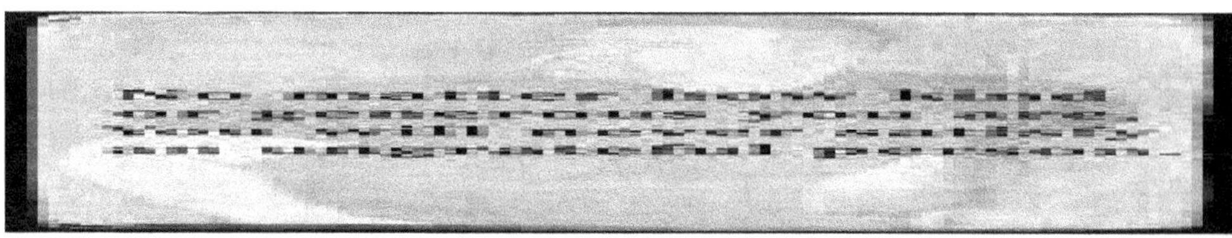

(They are never satisfied.)

PEOPLE WILL ALWAYS NOTICE THE CHANGE IN YOUR ATTITUDE TOWARDS THEM. BUT THEY WILL NEVER NOTICE IT'S THEIR BEHAVIOR WHICH MADE YOU CHANGE.

YOU ARE NOT REQUIRED
TO SET YOURSELF ON
FIRE TO KEEP OTHER
PEOPLE WARM.
UNKNOWN

CHAPTER ELEVEN
THE STORY OF FAIT

In the context of this literary work, the protagonist, whose identity is intentionally obfuscated as "Fait," originates from Nigeria. This individual's acquaintance arose through an intermediary, a young Gambian proprietor of an African establishment in Helsingborg, Sweden. Fait sought residential lodging, and the narrator, possessing a three-bedroom domicile, offered a room for rent.

Prior to Fait's introduction, the narrator engaged in a discourse with an unnamed confidant who had prior knowledge of Fait. The confidant divulged details of Fait's character, painting a somewhat controversial portrait. However, the narrator remained unperturbed, preferring to form their own opinions based on personal observations rather than second-hand accounts.

Subsequently, Fait took up residence in the narrator's apartment, and their cohabitation commenced. The initial week passed uneventfully, with the narrator maintaining a vigilant presence during their time at home. The narrator's work schedule consisted of Monday through Friday, leaving weekends available for leisure.

During this period of observation, the narrator witnessed the gradual manifestation of traits previously described by the confidant. As days transitioned into weeks, the characteristics attributed to Fait unfolded, aligning with the earlier characterization.

Ms. Fiat, a resident of Sweden, was experiencing prolonged telephone conversations with her husband residing in Nigeria. The nature of these conversations often involved heated arguments that disrupted the household's tranquillity.

Unable to endure the disturbance any longer, the narrator approached Ms. Fiat to express concerns about the nocturnal disruptions. During a morning conversation, Ms. Fiat confides in the narrator, revealing that her marital situation was tumultuous. She had entered a marriage that was not in her best interests. Her husband was exploiting her to facilitate his immigration to Sweden.

Ms. Fiat narrates her involvement with her husband. They met online when he was living in Turkey and unemployed.

He engaged in fraudulent activities online. Ms. Fiat had been assisting him by using her personal account to receive payments from clients. After hearing Ms. Fiat's account, the narrator expresses sympathy and provides guidance. That emphasize the potential legal and financial risks of participating in fraudulent activities. He also advises Ms. Fiat to seek employment and become financially independent rather than rely solely on her husband's financial assistance.

The next day, Ms. Fiat receives a call from the bank regarding a suspicious deposit made into her account. She informs the narrator and expresses apprehension about visiting the bank. The narrator advises her to cooperate and provide an explanation.

Ms. Fiat follows the narrator's advice and visits the bank. Upon her return, she informs the narrator about her interaction. The narrator reiterates the importance of discontinuing such activities while residing in the narrator's property.

Ms. Fiat's husband, dependent on her financial assistance, becomes aware of the narrator's intervention. The narrator speaks with the husband, advising him to support Ms. Fiat's efforts to pursue employment or relocate to the United Kingdom, where she would have greater opportunities.

Subsequently, she acquiesced to the narrator counsel and expressed a need for assistance in relocating to the United Kingdom. However, she lacked access to accommodations or support in applying for the EU Pre-settlement Scheme, which would authorize her employment and residency in the United Kingdom.

The narrator extended his assistance in various aspects, including contacting a long-standing acquaintance residing in Colchester. With unflagging support, the narrators friend graciously offered her address to facilitate the pre-settlement application process. The application was expeditiously completed, culminating in the successful approval of her pre-settlement status.

Nevertheless, a significant hurdle remained: her financial constraints hindered her relocation. She faced the dual obligation of settling her rent in Sweden and covering her initial month's rent in the United Kingdom.

Prior to her relocation to the United Kingdom, her spouse had expressed concerns about the influence of the narrator on Fiat and advised her to distance herself and relocate far away from the narrator's residence. She subsequently conveyed her decision to relocate with the intention of mitigating further conflict. However, despite her departure, the discord persisted due to her adherence to my counsel regarding the unauthorized use of her personal account for her husband's financial transactions.

On a notable Sunday, she initiated contact and inquired about the narrator's presence at home. Upon the narrator affirmative response, she indicated her imminent arrival within approximately twenty minutes. Upon her arrival, she proceeded to disclose her reasons for seeking assistance. She acknowledged a pressing need for support and identified the narrator as the sole individual capable of providing it.

She requested the narrator's assistance in securing a loan from a financial institution, with the promise of repayment once she had secured employment in the United Kingdom. The narrator declined, redirecting her to her spouse for financial support. She expressed her husband's disapproval of her relocation plans and his preference for her to remain in Sweden. However, she had firmly rejected his counsel.

Recognizing the need for self-reliance, she declined to avail herself of her husband's fraudulent assistance. Despite the narrator's initial reluctance to aid her, a sense of remorse prompted the narrator to reconsider. Upon inviting her to the narrator residence, she presented her laptop, enabling them to execute an online loan application. The approval was swift, and they mutually agreed to repay the loan. However, subsequent interactions revealed her growing entitlement. Her accusations of financial deceit, without any basis in fact, indicated a troubling lack of gratitude. This early manifestation served as a foreboding of her future conduct, which would ultimately confirm her ingratitude as an associate.

Upon receipt of the formally executed loan agreement, the financial disbursement was promptly effectuated. Subsequently, the narrator remitted her portion of the funds to her designated account. Surprisingly for the narrator, she recontacted him, expressing contrition for her prior scepticism regarding his judgment. The narrator elected to refrain from further dialogue. Simultaneously, she initiated the necessary preparations for her relocation.

Approximately seven days later, she contacted the narrator, indicating her desire to visit his residence. Her purpose was to request his assistance in establishing various financial arrangements, including the automation of rent, utilities, insurance, and loan repayments. The narrator informed her that she was welcome to visit on either Saturday or Sunday.

On Sunday, she arrived as scheduled while he was engaged in culinary endeavours in the kitchen. Upon inquiring if she desired sustenance, she affirmed her hunger. The narrator invited her to avail herself of the prepared meal.

In the confines of her solitude within the kitchen, the narrator presence was concealed behind a meticulously placed security camera, granting him remote access to her actions.

Unexpectedly, the camera captured an enigmatic moment: she extracted an unknown substance from underneath her breast area and surreptitiously attempted to conceal it within a cooking pot resting upon the stove.

Startled by the unfolding scene, the narrator's chose to enter the room, feigning nonchalance despite the palpable shock and awkwardness of the situation. As she hurriedly departed with her meal in hand, a myriad of questions raced through his mind, fuelling his curiosity about her motives.

Upon observing a sudden shift in the narrator's demeanour, she accelerated her consumption of food and swiftly exited the kitchen area. The narrator, feigning indifference, directed her to leave her utensils at the sink, intending to cleanse them himself.

Days later, the narrator confronted her, inquiring about her peculiar behaviour. After a moment of hesitation, she denied her actions, dismissing them as mere fabrications. However, the narrator presented irrefutable evidence of her misconduct, admonishing her to desist from any further unsavoury attempts.

From that day forward, she distanced herself from the narrator, her presence fading with the passing weeks. As her departure for the United Kingdom loomed, she reached out once more, seeking his assistance. Without hesitation, the narrator extended his support, despite the lingering doubts that clouded his mind.

Upon her arrival in the United Kingdom, a twist of fate forced the narrator to intervene when a trusted friend declined to provide accommodation for her. Faced with this unexpected turn of events, the narrator's resolve wavered, and she ultimately denied her request for accommodation as earlier planned.

Fate, as it so often does, intervened, and she found solace with an acquaintance from her homeland residing in Scotland.

In a twist of destiny, the narrator and the acquaintance crossed paths once again after the narrator's relocation to the United Kingdom from Sweden. She reached out to him, requesting assistance with her integration into the foreign system. Yet, as she navigated her new existence, parallels

continued to emerge, reminding the narrator of the
cautionary tales he had penned.

(Fait is another good of an ungrateful friend.)

VALUE AND APPRECIATE THE PEOPLE WHO
SACRIFICE THEIR ''SOMETHING'' FOR YOU.
BECAUSE MAYBE THAT ''SOMETHING'' WAS
THEIR EVERYTHING.

CHAPTER TWELVE

REBUILDING TRUST FOLLOWING BETRAYAL IS CRUCIAL AND DELICATE PROCESS

The Betrayal of Friendship

A prevalent form of betrayal within the realm of friendship occurs when an individual relinquishes their affinity with a close companion in favour of a newfound romantic relationship. This abrupt shift, marked by a cessation of shared experiences and companionship, can evoke a profound sense of devaluation and irrelevance for the abandoned friend.

Betrayal, in its broader context, encompasses instances where a friend fails to provide emotional support or physical presence in times of need. It can also manifest when a friendship is terminated unilaterally, leaving the aggrieved party longing for its continuation and often baffled as to its demise.

Ungrateful friends, driven by self-interest or envy, may betray the trust placed upon them. Their actions, often motivated by material gain or the promise of personal advancement, necessitate caution and the judicious avoidance of their company.

Reconstituting trust with individuals who have engaged in betrayal is a formidable endeavour. For those who have endured such a violation, be it infidelity, financial ruin, or emotional defamation, the path to rebuilding trust is arduous. However, the potential rewards are substantial. While betrayals are not always indicative of underlying relationship or friendship issues, they can serve as catalysts for self-reflection and the re-evaluation of one's social network. This introspection can ultimately mitigate the likelihood of future betrayals and pave the way for the restoration of trust.

Friendship transcends mere romantic entanglements or superficial congeniality. It necessitates a profound understanding of one's partner's interiority, encompassing their aspirations, motivations, and well-being.

Integral to friendship is the assumption of responsibility for errors, both minor and grave. A pivotal factor in restoring trust post-transgressions is not only love but also the capacity of both parties to acknowledge their respective contributions to the discord. This may be an onerous task, particularly for victims of betrayal. However, it is an indispensable step towards salvaging the relationship.

After establishing shared accountability, regaining a sense of control is paramount. It is predicated on the notion that individuals are not mere pawns of friendship's whims or their own missteps; rather, they possess the agency to mend the relationship. Consequently, the perpetrator must cede a measure of control to the victim, while the latter must endeavour to reclaim it.

Beyond these foundational principles, additional measures are crucial for the betrayed party:

- **Abjure Humiliation:** Resist the temptation to indulge in schadenfreude by subjecting your partner to public degradation. This dichotomy ultimately undermines the potential for reconciliation. By denying your partner the opportunity to atone, you increase the likelihood of irreparable harm to the relationship.
- **Embrace Empathy:** Consider the transgressor's perspective and endeavour to comprehend their motivations, however reprehensible. This not only fosters a spirit of compassion but also provides valuable insights into the underlying causes of the conflict.
- **Seek Professional Assistance:** If necessary, do not hesitate to consult with a qualified therapist or

- counsellor. An impartial third party can provide objective guidance and facilitate constructive communication between the parties.
- Effective communication in friendship repair entails separating legitimate complaints from counterproductive criticism. Complaints that focus on specific behaviours, expressed in a manner that inspires a desire to rebuild trust, promote healing.
- Avoid expressing criticisms that induce shame, humiliation, or fault-finding. These negative emotions foster defensiveness and impede progress. Researcher Martin Seligman advocates for recognizing that flaws in friends are often situational rather than inherent. For instance, consider the betrayal as a regretful incident, acknowledging your own potential contributions rather than attributing it to an underlying character defect. Such a perspective facilitates forgiveness.
- **Establishing Boundaries for Betrayal Discussions**
- Resist the impulse to dwell constantly on the betrayal. Excessive focus can harm both parties. Acknowledge the restorative power of distraction and establish a designated time for brief daily check-ins to address the matter. The betrayed individual should control the frequency of these conversations.
- **Assessing Forgiveness Capacity**

- Evaluate the severity of the wound and the betrayer's capacity for change. If the betrayal is part of a pattern of untrustworthiness, it may be prudent to question whether restoring trust is feasible.
- Furthermore, assess the betrayer's genuine commitment to rehabilitation. Emotional biases may cloud your ability to interpret their words. Nevertheless, regaining a sense of control, even if it deviates from traditional friendship norms, is essential. Consider reviewing communication logs to establish congruence between words and actions.
- **Making Amends as the Betrayer**
- Those who have betrayed a loved one often grapple with guilt, sadness, and low self-esteem. Acknowledging one's responsibility for the actions, regardless of the perceived justifications, is paramount. Avoid blaming the betrayed party, as this prolongs their healing process.
- Anticipate a lengthy recovery period for the betrayed individual. Demonstrate empathy and willingness to endure ongoing discussions about the betrayal. External support from close associates or a therapist may be necessary.

Acknowledge and confront the discomfort associated with witnessing the impact of your actions on others. Demonstrate empathy by actively listening to the expressions of pain and disappointment, understanding their emotions, and assuming responsibility for causing them.

Respecting Boundaries and Transparency

Recognize the need for enhanced transparency and accountability to rebuild trust. Embrace the establishment of new boundaries and rules, such as increased accessibility to communication records. A cooperative and non-defensive approach will facilitate healing and the restoration of trust.

Commitment to Change and Repair

Demonstrate a genuine desire for personal transformation and relationship repair. Beyond seeking therapeutic support, consider significant actions such as altering employment or relocating as evidence of a long-term commitment to restoration.

(Betrayal of trust is difficult to understand)

CHAPTER THIRTEEN

COPING WITH THE BETRAYAL OF TRUST

Have you ever experienced the sting of betrayal?

This insidious experience, which I have encountered both personally and professionally, has an uncanny propensity to manifest amongst those we hold most dear - individuals whose trustworthiness we assume implicitly.

In the aftermath of betrayal, a torrent of emotions may surge through the psyche: anger, resentment, and a profound sense of violation. Questions race through the mind: Should I confront the perpetrator? Expose their treachery? How can I navigate this treacherous path?

While individual responses to betrayal vary, a crucial distinction lies in the choice to overcome its negative impact in a constructive or destructive manner. It may seem paradoxical to approach such a profoundly adverse experience with a positive outlook, yet it is an attainable feat.

As one who has successfully navigated this arduous journey, I present five fundamental beliefs that anchored my recovery:

Engage with the Source of Disappointment

Perspectives vary significantly. A perceived transgression may stem from a misinterpretation rather than an intentional act. Thus, it is imperative to engage with the individual involved. Inquire about their interpretation of events, seeking clarity and understanding.

Allow for Explanations

Suppressing frustrations is counterproductive when a misunderstanding could be the underlying cause. Holding onto resentment or negative sentiments can negatively impact other relationships.

Maintain Emotional Elevation

Aspire to embody a higher consciousness, focusing on self-improvement and contentment. Avoid actions born out of a mindset associated with lower emotional frequencies.

Preserve Inner Well-being

Confronting a perceived betrayal should not compromise your emotional well-being. Maintain a positive and constructive mindset, refraining from exposing or harbouring ill will towards the other party.

Prioritize Personal Growth

Allocate your energy towards self-development and the realization of your aspirations. Dwell on positive thoughts and actions, avoiding unnecessary expenditure of time and energy on negative events.

Adhere to Universal Principles

Remember that actions have consequences, and what is put out into the world is reciprocated. Align your conduct with your values and purpose, making decisions that reflect your highest self. Let those who act dishonourably bear the consequences of their own actions.

Embrace the Treachery

Contemplate the transgression with equanimity. Engage in introspective inquiry, seeking enlightenment from the unwelcome experience.

The betrayal served a profound purpose: to impart invaluable lessons and propel you towards personal growth. Should the burden of resentment prove

insurmountable, resort to a cathartic act of schrift:
transcribe your frustrations onto parchment, then consign it
to the purifying flames.

Regardless of your chosen path, the imperative remains to
relinquish the grip of negativity. Yet, before doing so,
glean the wisdom embedded within its embrace.

UNGRATEFUL PEOPLE COMPLAIN
ABOUT THE ONE THING YOU
HAVEN'T DONE FOR THEM
INSTEAD OF BEING THANKFUL
FOR THE THOUSANDS OF THINGS
YOU HAVE DONE FOR THEM.
DON'T INVEST YOUR TIME INTO
PEOPLE WHO THINK IT'S YOUR
OBLIGATION TO CURE THEIR ILLS.

OE

CHAPTER FOURTEEN

STRATEGIES FOR HANDLING UNGRATEFUL INDIVIDUALS

The Deleterious Effects of Ungrateful Associations

Ungratefulness, an insidious trait, can exert a profoundly negative influence upon one's well-being. Constant exposure to individuals devoid of appreciation for the blessings they possess, and the kindnesses extended to them can have a detrimental impact, potentially fostering dissatisfaction or even irritability.

For those entangled in such relationships, characterized by a perpetual cycle of giving and receiving without reciprocation, it is imperative to adopt a series of precautionary measures:

Introspection and Self-Affirmation

Engage in self-reflection, identifying triggers that elicit feelings of dissatisfaction. Examine underlying beliefs about self-worth and determine if the absence of gratitude from others is interpreted as a reflection of inadequacy.

Affirm your inherent value, regardless of external validation. Cultivate a belief in your worthiness and unwavering sense of self-esteem. If instilled during childhood, such knowledge can empower individuals throughout their lives.

Granting the Benefit of the Doubt

Acknowledge that individuals may be grappling with personal challenges that hinder their expression of gratitude. Recognize that people often respond to life's circumstances based on learned behaviours and past experiences.

Initiating Dialogue

Should residual concerns persist after considering potential mitigating factors, it is prudent to initiate a conversation to address the issue. Timeliness is crucial to prevent the accumulation of negative emotions.

Remember that a constructive dialogue involves reciprocal communication. If this proves unfeasible, consider expressing your feelings through written correspondence or private reflection.

Assertiveness and Boundaries

Exercise your right to decline requests or distance yourself from individuals who exhibit a chronic pattern of ingratitude. While aspirational to adopt a selfless approach, it is important to recognize that some individuals will never be satisfied. Their behaviour is often a reflection of their own self-perception, not a deficiency in your character.

Establish clear boundaries to protect your time and energy. Prioritize activities that align with your own desires and values.

Non-Attachment

Recognize the futility of attempting to control the behaviour or thought processes of others. Engage in interactions without expectations of reciprocation or specific outcomes. By relinquishing attachment to the result, you can liberate yourself from potential disappointment.

Introspection: Assessing One's Own Deficiency

In moments of perceived ingratitude, it is paramount to redirect our focus inward. The act of "dealing" with others is, in essence, a reflection of our own inner needs and beliefs. By understanding this fundamental truth, we can embark on a transformative journey towards self-fulfilments.

Embracing Self-Reliance

The pursuit of happiness should not be contingent upon external validation. We have the inherent power to cultivate a state of contentment and gratitude that transcends the need for others to fill our void. By detaching our sense of well-being from the actions or reactions of others, we empower ourselves to live authentic and purpose-driven lives.

Examining Negative Thought Patterns

Unhappiness often stems from a mindset of lack and blame, a perspective that perpetuates a cycle of negativity. Instead of expending our energy on fruitless attempts to change others, we must focus on transforming ourselves. By replacing negative thoughts with positive affirmations and visualizations, we reprogram our subconscious minds, which exert a profound influence on our overall well-being.

Recognizing the Power of Perspective

It is essential to approach others with empathy and compassion, recognizing that their actions may stem from their own unique struggles. Rather than harbouring resentment or judgment, we should embrace the imperfections of human nature and seek to understand the underlying motivations of those who may appear ungrateful.

The Importance of Self-Reflection

Daily introspection is a cornerstone of personal growth. By asking ourselves, "How can I change my negative programming today? How can I replace my negative thinking with happiness?" we embark on a path of self-discovery and continuous improvement.

Summary

True happiness resides not in grand gestures or distant milestones, but in the accumulation of countless small moments of contentment. By mastering our own thoughts and cultivating a mindset of self-reliance and gratitude, we transcend the limitations imposed by others and unlock the boundless potential within ourselves.

Navigating Negativity and Toxic Personalities

Transforming individuals can be a protracted and arduous endeavour, particularly if your commitment to their growth is lacking. Hence, embarking on such an undertaking is not advisable unless you are fully invested. Furthermore, if the likelihood of future interactions is minimal, it is prudent to refrain from attempts at altering their behaviour. As the adage goes, "Sometimes it's best to let go."

Resist the urge to confront those who exhibit discourtesy, such as failing to acknowledge gestures of gratitude. While your frustration may be understandable, succumbing to such impulses can only lead to unproductive confrontations.

For individuals who do not fall into the categories, consider employing a strategy of gratitude to neutralize their negativity. Regardless of their actions or demeanour, seek opportunities to express appreciation toward them.

For instance, if a colleague fails to express gratitude for a meticulously prepared spreadsheet, acknowledge their trust in your abilities and the knowledge gained during its creation. Similarly, if a close acquaintance fails to appreciate your assistance with childcare, express gratitude for the opportunity to interact with their children.

Such actions may have an insignificant impact on the other party, or they may go unnoticed entirely. However, the repeated practice of gratitude will undoubtedly strengthen your own well-being. Research has demonstrated the incompatibility of negative thoughts and genuine feelings of thankfulness.

In extreme cases, it may be necessary to remove toxic individuals from your life. While this decision can be challenging, remember that their negative influence can ultimately undermine your own happiness and well-being.

If the situation reaches this point, it is imperative to prioritize your own well-being and seek external support if necessary. Leaving toxic relationships can be arduous, but it is an investment in your future well-being.

It is important to emphasize that the decision to remain or depart from negative situations is ultimately a personal choice. Regardless of the path you choose, it is essential to protect your own integrity and prioritize your own happiness. By doing so, you break free from the confines of others' negative behaviour and forge a path toward a more fulfilling life.

Ungrateful people
complain about the
one thing you haven't
done for them instead
of being thankful for
the thousands of
things you have done
for them.

CHAPTER FIFTEEN-

SIGNS OF AN UNGRATEFUL PEOPLE

Everlasting Dissatisfaction and Ingratitude

Individuals prone to perpetual dissatisfaction possess an unquenchable thirst for fulfilment. Despite achieving significant milestones and material possessions, they remain perpetually discontented. Their relentless pursuit of external validation eclipses their capacity for contentment and precludes gratitude for their current blessings.

Envy and Resentment

These individuals harbour a profound sense of envy, coveting the accomplishments and possessions of others. Their comparisons to others cast their own lives in an unfavourable light, fuelling an insatiable desire for what they perceive as superior. This envy corrodes their well-being, rendering them incapable of appreciating their own circumstances.

Bitterness and Entitlement

A lingering sense of bitterness permeates their interactions with the world. Past grievances and present misfortunes feed their resentment, fostering an inflated sense of entitlement. They expect unwavering support and favours from others, considering them a birthright rather than a privilege.

Constant Dependency and Unrequited Expectations

Ungrateful individuals exhibit a remarkable lack of self-reliance, perpetually seeking assistance from others. Their reliance on external aid stems from a misguided belief that they deserve preferential treatment. They fail to recognize the value of gratitude, expecting others to fulfil their requests without acknowledgment.

Disregard for Others

Their self-centeredness renders them oblivious to the needs of others. Empathy is foreign to them, as they prioritize their own well-being above all else. Relationships are reduced to transactional exchanges, with their presence contingent upon the fulfilment of their desires.

Victimhood Complex and Resistance to Change

These individuals adopt a perpetual victim mentality, perceiving themselves as perpetually wronged. They deflect responsibility for their circumstances, blaming external factors for their misfortunes. When confronted with constructive criticism or advice, they reflexively dismiss it, reinforcing their negative self-image.

The Consequences of Ungrateful Behaviour

Their ingratitude isolates them from others, depriving them of the support and respect they crave. Their relentless pursuit of external validation ultimately leaves them perpetually unfulfilled. The true cost of their attitude lies in the forfeiture of genuine human connection and the diminished joy that comes from appreciating the present moment.

CHAPTER SIXTEEN

71 UNGRATEFUL METHODS

In the realm of human interactions, encounters with ungrateful individuals are inevitable. While unintentional in nature, our own emotions can cloud our perception of the situation, making it challenging to maintain a balanced perspective.

For some individuals, however, ingratitude is a persistent pattern, often driven by underlying feelings of bitterness, envy, and frustration. Their incessant complaints and self-pitying demeanours can drain our energy and make their presence undesirable.

It is crucial to recognize that certain people will remain perpetually ungrateful, regardless of the sacrifices we make. They may habitually begrudge the blessings in their lives, fail to appreciate acts of kindness, and remain oblivious to the extent of our efforts on their behalf.

Whether it be in the workplace, among friends, or within our own families, the relentless negativity of ungrateful individuals can have a profound impact on our well-being. It is therefore imperative to establish boundaries and prioritize our own emotional well-being.

Quotes that Illuminating the Emotional Toll of Ungrateful Individuals:

"The person you are making sacrifices for will turn around and tell you they didn't ask you to, and they will be right."

Strategies for Dealing with Ungrateful Individuals:

1. "The unnoticed value of our actions becomes apparent when they cease." - Mike Skinner
2. "Unyielding ingratitude surpasses the malleability of stone." - South
3. "Happiness embraces selfless giving, forgiveness, and gratitude. The self-absorbed and ungrateful will remain perpetually unhappy." - Joseph Fort Newton
4. "The abode of the unappreciative." - Spanish Proverb
5. "My worthiness extends beyond mere utility." - Unknown
6. "Sacrifices are met with a denial of obligation." - Unknown
7. "Various forms of ingratitude exist denial, concealment, non-reciprocity, and oblivion." - Seneca the Younger

8. "Withdraw support when expectations replace appreciation." - Unknown
9. "My demeanour reflects the consequences of your actions." - Unknown
10. "Ungrateful hearts accompany moral depravity." - Miguel de Cervantes
11. "Ingrates are oblivious to the source of their sustenance." - Timothy Dexter
12. "Ingratitude creates a receptacle riddled with deficiencies." - Latin Proverb
13. "Happiness eludes the ungrateful." - Zig Ziglar
14. "Our selflessness and determination empower us to achieve extraordinary feats, despite adversity and ingratitude." - Mother Teresa
15. "Scrutinize your priorities when your efforts are met with indifference." - Unknown
16. "Time is a precious resource not to be squandered on the ungrateful." - Scottie Waves
17. "Ingratitude tarnishes all virtues." - Edward Young
18. "Recognize the limits of your sacrifices and withdraw from relationships that lack reciprocity." - Unknown
19. "Gratitude alleviates the burden of sorrow." - Tom Krause

20. "Cultivate gratitude for the blessings in your life, regardless of their magnitude. Appreciate the fragility of existence and count your blessings, for there are those who strive valiantly for what you may take for granted." – Unknown
21. **Maintain composure and disregard those who exhibit ingratitude.** - Read Beach
22. **Numerous sources of gratitude exist in the realm of existence. Let not a single instance of ingratitude mar your experience.** - Unknown
23. **Individuals tend to disregard countless acts of assistance, recalling solely the omission of a single request.** - Unknown
24. **Some individuals will attempt to diminish your reputation and present you as unappreciative, despite your significant contributions to their well-being.** - Unknown
25. **Cultivate the practice of withholding your presence from those who fail to acknowledge its value.** - Unknown
26. **The ungrateful consistently overlook a multitude of acts of kindness, recalling only the occasion when their requests were denied.** - Abdulbary Yahya
27. **The level of ingratitude among people is astonishing. They fail to express appreciation for**

the restraint I exercise in refraining from fatal
actions. – Unknown

28. A single ungrateful individual can inflict harm
upon all those who require assistance. - Publilius
Syrus
29. Abundant blessings and sources of gratitude
exist. Allow not a single instance of ingratitude to
overshadow your spirit. - Unknown
30. A tongue that incessantly complains is indicative
of a heart devoid of gratitude. - William Arthur
Ward
31. Efforts directed towards the ungrateful are
ultimately wasted. - Seneca The Younger
32. Fulfil your obligations through acts of giving,
even when gratitude is scarce. - Unknown
33. Cherish and value all that you possess. - Benjamin
Disraeli
34. One is not obligated to sacrifice one's well-being
for the comfort of others. - Unknown
35. Extending kindness to the ungrateful is akin to
pouring rosewater into the boundless sea. - Latin
Proverb
36. Gratitude enriches the heart with contentment,
while ingratitude perpetuates a state of
dissatisfaction. - David A. Bednar

37. **Refrain from assisting the ungrateful in their recovery. It is tantamount to informing a predator of your vulnerability.** - Unknown

38. **A complaining tongue is the manifestation of an ungrateful heart.** - William Arthur Ward

39. **Recognize the necessity of establishing boundaries and withdrawing support from those who do not reciprocate.** - Unknown

40. **Gratitude and contentment are the true measures of wealth.** - Tony Robbins

41. **The ungrateful have the ability to provoke extreme reactions. However, it is crucial to maintain composure in the face of adversity.** - Unknown

42. **Compassion should not be extended to the ungrateful, as they may lack understanding or experience.** - Chico Xavier

43. Embittering sentiments arise towards those who exhibit a profound lack of appreciation. Despite the utmost efforts to elicit their contentment, their desires remain unsated. (Anonymous)

44. Extreme benevolence may invite exploitation. Those extended succour may find themselves subjected to ungracious complaints about perceived inadequacies. (Anonymous)

45. Strive for excellence in all endeavours but avoid the pitfall of ingratitude. Cherish the blessings bestowed upon you. (Anonymous)
46. While human nature may occasionally falter in expressing gratitude, the totality of mankind retains the capacity for acknowledgment. (John Milton)
47. Perpetual negativity and a void of appreciation are highly detrimental to one's well-being and presence. (Anonymous)
48.**48.** Chronic gratitude deficiency manifests as a communicable malaise known as unhappiness. (Mokokoma Mokhonoana)
49. When expectations of reciprocal assistance replace appreciation, it is prudent to reassess relationships. (Kush and Wizdom)
50. Embrace the awareness of one's imperfections while acknowledging the abundance of blessings. (Zig Ziglar)
51. Disillusionment may arise when witnessing the ingratitude of those to whom one has extended aid. (Anonymous)
52. The absence of gratitude blinds individuals to the blessings that enrich their lives. (Anonymous)
53. Exploitation occurs only with the acquiescence of its victims. (Anonymous)
54. The most heinous vice is ingratitude. (Anonymous)

55. Repeated assistance may foster a sense of entitlement, leading to ungrateful attitudes. (Anonymous)
56. Gratitude, a rare and precious virtue, is often lacking in all strata of society. (Wilkie Collins)
57. Avoid disappointment by recognizing that not all individuals possess the same capacity for empathy and gratitude. (Anonymous)
58. Forgive the occasional lapse in decorum, but do not tolerate chronic rudeness. (Anonymous)
59. Ingratitude and inconsideration are deeply irksome. While extending favours is commendable, it is essential to guard against being taken advantage of. (Anonymous)
60. Ingratitude is akin to a corrosive force that erodes one's soul, blinding them to the beauty and wonder of life. (Geraldine Vermaak)
61. Happiness eludes those who fail to appreciate the present moment. (Anonymous)
62. Discretion should be exercised in determining those worthies of one's kindness. (Anonymous)
63. Avoid setting excessive expectations, as they often pave the way for disappointment. (Ryan Reynolds)
64. Surround yourself with individuals who foster positive qualities, such as gratitude, kindness, and ambition. (Germany Kent)

65. The true extent of one's contributions is often overlooked, while the slightest omission is magnified. (Anonymous)
66. Selfishness breeds ingratitude. (Lailah Gifty Akita)
67. Ungrateful individuals contribute to a toxic environment. Generosity, on the other hand, promotes growth and prosperity. (Paul McCabe)
68.
69. Solitude is preferable to the company of those who fail to recognize one's value. (Nishan Panwar)
70. Human nature dictates that individuals acknowledge shifts in others' attitudes but fail to recognize their own behaviours as the catalysts for such transformations. (Not Salmon)
71. Protect your inner peace by distancing yourself from ungrateful individuals. Sometimes, the absence of presence is the most effective means of fostering respect. (Tony A. Gaskins, Jr.)
72. Gratitude should be an intrinsic aspect of all relationships. (Anonymous)

Summary:

It is essential to differentiate between isolated instances of ingratitude and chronic patterns of thanklessness. While occasional grumbling is inevitable, it is unwarranted to allow such negativity to deplete one's energy. Recognize your self-worth and seek the company of those who genuinely appreciate your presence. Remember the blessings in your life and strive to foster an environment of gratitude and positivity.

CHAPTER SEVENTEEN

HABITS OF HIGHLY UNGRATEFUL PEOPLE

The Lesson of Ungrateful Souls: Compassion and Resilience

While ungrateful individuals may exploit generosity and leave one feeling abandoned and exploited, it is imperative to recognize that even those who exhibit such negative traits can serve as valuable life instructors.

Characteristics of Ungrateful Individuals

These perpetually dissatisfied individuals perceive the world through a distorted lens, failing to appreciate the positive aspects of their lives. This insatiable yearning for fulfilment perpetuates a sense of emptiness.

They perceive themselves as entitled, often stemming from a history of adversity. This belief creates a perceived obligation on others to compensate for their perceived injustices.

Their bitterness manifests as a proclivity for anger and resentment. They dwell on past grievances and criticize the

present, making it challenging to engage meaningfully with them.

They adopt the mantle of victimhood, believing they face insurmountable obstacles. Despite external support, they resist change, seeking to maintain their perceived status.

Overcoming Their Impact

To mitigate the negative effects of such individuals, it is crucial to cultivate appreciation for the present moment and the small gestures of kindness that fill our lives.

Remember that all individuals are on equal footing, regardless of their circumstances. Entitlement should be replaced with a sense of mutual respect.

Emphasize compassion over judgment. By stepping into their perspective, we can foster deeper understanding and empathy.

Instead of dwelling on weaknesses, embrace resilience. Adversity builds inner strength and offers valuable life lessons.

Finally, recognize that not everyone is genuinely concerned about our well-being. It is important to establish

boundaries and protect oneself from those who seek to exploit kindness.

Self-Centred Individuals

Individuals who prioritize their own interests exclusively exhibit a profound lack of empathy towards the sentiments and well-being of others. Their preoccupation with self-preservation and strategic planning eclipses any consideration for the needs of others.

Counterproductive Behaviours

Rather than emulating their self-centred nature, it is imperative to prioritize compassion and empathy. By exhibiting such virtues, one not only experiences personal fulfilment but also fosters a positive environment, regardless of its impact on the individuals.

The Perils of Ingratitude

Individuals who perpetually maintain a negative perspective are often immersed in excessive distractions and noise, such as constant communication, excessive commitments, and relentless obligations. This constant bombardment can hinder their ability to appreciate the

positive aspects of life, fostering a sense of entitlement and ingratitude.

Gratitude and Fulfilment

Expressions of gratitude stem from a genuine sense of contentment and well-being. Individuals who acknowledge and appreciate what they possess cultivate a heightened awareness of their blessings and a profound appreciation for life's experiences.

Fear and Economic Loss

Fear can serve as a catalyst for ingratitude, driving individuals to engage in unfulfilling work and relationships out of a misguided sense of security. This perpetual state of worry can lead to physical ailments, emotional distress, and social isolation.

Greed and Generosity

Highly ungrateful individuals often exhibit stinginess and a lack of generosity, motivated by a fear of economic loss. This mindset manifests in a preoccupation with financial concerns, obscuring their ability to experience joy and fulfilment in life.

Conflict and Insecurity

Unstable and insecure individuals may engage in unnecessary conflicts to assert their dominance or maintain a sense of control over their surroundings. These conflicts are often rooted in irrational thoughts and serve as a means of externalizing their own negative emotions.

Secondly, they anticipate reciprocation in the form of compassion and understanding. Failure to adhere to their expectations evokes prompt denouncement. However, should the issue be raised once more, they adeptly feign ignorance, asserting that the purported incident never transpired. Skilfully manoeuvring the narrative, they portray themselves as injured parties, despite their instigation of the conflict.

Highly ungrateful individuals engage in blame allocation and victimization. They attribute their perceived shortcomings to parental upbringing, childhood victimization, or interpersonal conflicts. Tenaciously clinging to these grievances, they tirelessly pursue the blame game.

A pervasive negativity taints their interpretation of human interactions. They misinterpret remarks, comments, and

opinions, perceiving insidious undertones of insult, belittlement, or disparagement. This unwavering belief in the dishonourable intentions of others fosters distrust, resentment, and a constant defensive stance.

Self-absorption characterizes their mindset. Their unwavering focus on personal needs and problems overshadows the concerns of others. They brood over their motivations, behaviours', and shortcomings, perpetuating a cycle of self-criticism and preoccupation.

Unmitigated ingratitude manifests as incessant criticism. Nothing meets their standards, leaving them perpetually discontented. Their negative outlook permeates their interactions, discordantly opposing the opinions of others. They eagerly voice their criticisms, seeking to draw attention to their perspective. Antagonism and a false sense of infallibility drive their words, while undermining the achievements and sentiments of others.

Their insidious envy of others' successes betrays their true nature. While not explicitly acknowledging their feelings, they subtly diminish the accomplishments of others by highlighting negatives or downplaying their significance, effectively extinguishing the other person's exhilaration. In moments of others' joy, highly ungrateful individuals

meticulously enumerate potential pitfalls, casting a pall on the occasion.

The inherent pessimism of ungrateful individuals clouds their perception of the future. They subscribe to the notion that life is rife with adversity and that optimism is futile. Their pessimistic outlook casts doubt on the longevity of relationships, the love of their children, the integrity of their homes, and the sanctity of their employment.

"Individuals exhibit a proclivity for engaging in interpersonal conflicts both within their own sphere and beyond. They assume a central role in the propagation of drama, often fomenting discord among family members and community members. Their desire for attention manifests itself through a willingness to commiserate with others who harbour feelings of discontent. They contribute to the escalation of emotional turmoil by exaggerating situations and providing a sympathetic ear to those who express dissatisfaction with their circumstances, thereby perpetuating a cycle of negativity and reinforcing the notion that life treats them unjustly."

If you heal the leg
of a person, do
not be surprise if
they use it to run
away.

- African Proverb

CHAPTER EIGHTEEN

PERFECT SCENARIO OF UNGRATEFULS

Upon an exhaustive examination of the narratives pertaining to Edingo, Asino, Fait, and Lukewell, an irrefutable conclusion emerges they serve as exemplary archetypes of individuals exhibiting a profound deficiency in the virtue of gratitude. Their utterances and deeds unequivocally attest to the veracity of this assertion, rendering them exemplars of those who warrant meticulous scrutiny in the tapestry of our daily interactions.

Do a good deed
and throw it into
the sea.

– African Proverb

A snake was hit by a car. A
woman picks him up, feeds
him, & gets him to a full state
of health. But then he bites
her, injecting her with his
deadly venom. On her death
bed, she asked "after all I did,
why me?" The snake says,
"you knew I was a snake when
you picked me up!"

(The reality of life)

CHAPTER NINETEEN

SOME OF THE ROOT CAUSE OF
UNGRATEFULNESS

Manifestations of Ungrateful Individuals

Certain individuals exhibit ungrateful tendencies, which
may include:

- Limited empathy and consideration for others
- An inflated sense of self-importance, believing they
  are the sole focus of attention
- An expectation that others are obligated to "serve"
  them for their own benefit
- Persistent feelings of envy and dissatisfaction
- Difficulty expressing their true feelings and
  experiences

Addressing Ungrateful behaviours

To address ungrateful behaviours, consider the following
approach:

- **Emphasize your perspective:** Utilize "I" statements
  to convey how their actions affect you, stating, for
-

- instance, "I feel my assistance is often taken for granted, despite my absence of obligation."
- **Maintain firmness and openness:** Assertively communicate your stance while also providing opportunities for them to respond and provide their perspective.
- **Highlight the consequences:** Discuss how their ingratitude can hinder their well-being, leading to resentment and dissatisfaction.

Psychological Implications of Ungrateful behaviours

Ungrateful individuals tend to concentrate on life's negative aspects, neglecting the positive. This myopic mindset can perpetuate a cycle of negativity and dissatisfaction. Moreover, ingratitude inhibits the expression of appreciation, which is essential for building meaningful relationships.

Gratitude as a Path to Fulfilment

True gratitude involves recognizing the positive aspects of life and appreciating the contributions of others. Practicing gratitude promotes a positive mindset, enhances well-being, and fosters resilience in the face of adversity. It is a key ingredient for cultivating happiness and contentment.

Understanding Ungrateful behaviours in Children

Occasionally, children display ungrateful behaviour not out of a lack of appreciation but rather a subconscious resistance to relying solely on others for their needs. This complex emotion reflects a sense of independence and maturity that may be emerging in them.

The Essence of Gratitude

Gratitude is the heartfelt acknowledgment of the good in one's life. It recognizes the tangible and intangible benefits received. Cultivating gratitude promotes positivity, enhanced experiences, improved health, and the formation of strong bonds. It is a virtue that enriches both the giver and the recipient, fostering a sense of connection and fulfilment.

Gratitude transcends mere intellectual comprehension; it demands a visceral experience. Amidst the ebb and flow of life, pause, inhale deeply, and offer a silent acknowledgment to the gift of existence. This practice transcends the need for specific beneficiaries or explicit reasons.

The antithesis of gratitude lies not only in ungratefulness, but also in unappreciation. Ungratefulness denotes a

deficiency in acknowledging kindness, while unappreciation reflects a broader lack of gratitude.

As elucidated by the Cambridge Dictionary, gratitude encompasses "an intense sentiment of appreciation for an individual or entity's beneficence." When gratitude eludes us, we erect barriers to the free exchange of love.

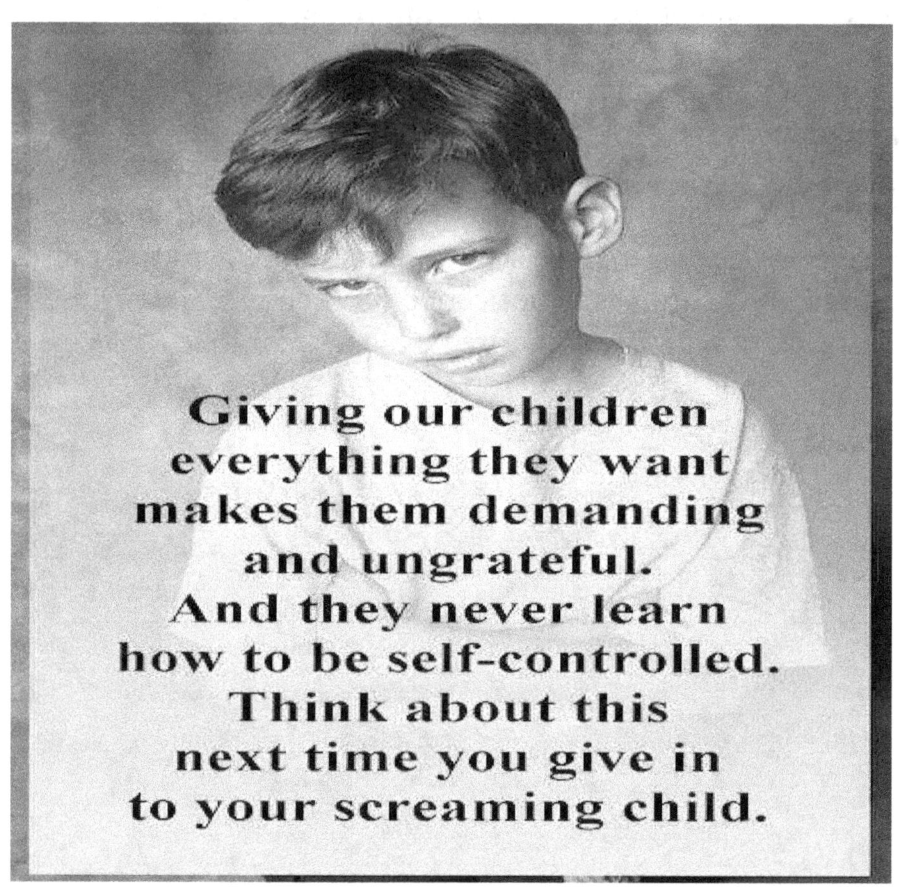

Giving our children
everything they want
makes them demanding
and ungrateful.
And they never learn
how to be self-controlled.
Think about this
next time you give in
to your screaming child.

104

CHAPTER TWENTY

AUTHORS CONCLUSION

In summation, we must cultivate an attitude of profound gratitude for the benevolent actions extended towards us, whether directed at ourselves or those within our immediate sphere of relationships, including kin, confidants, and offspring. Gratitude is an intrinsic moral imperative, acknowledged by the divine and conducive to our overall well-being.

Conversely, the absence of due recognition or expressions of appreciation engenders dissatisfaction and discouragement, fostering a sense of unfulfillment among those who labour tirelessly. It obstructs divine favour, damages interpersonal bonds, and impedes access to future benefits.

Gratitude, a profound sentiment of thankfulness and appreciation, manifests with a myriad of health advantages, both mental and physical. Its essence lies in acknowledging the presence of beneficence in one's life, accompanied by feelings of kindness, warmth, and benevolence in response.

The concept of gratitude assumes diverse interpretations depending on its context and usage. Generally, it denotes an awareness of fortunate circumstances, coupled with an attribution of agency to an external source, whether human or non-human, such as nature or a spiritual entity.

Philosophers and theologians have pondered the nature of gratitude since antiquity. Empirical research emerged in the mid-20th century as scholars explored the impact of gratitude on individuals and communities. The topic has garnered increasing attention due to its evident implications for well-being.

Expressions of gratitude are multifaceted, encompassing various forms, such as:

Assessment of Gratitude

Quantifying one's inherent proclivity for gratitude necessitates introspection via a series of pertinent inquiries:

- Do you perceive an abundance of blessings in your life?
- Is the enumeration of your gratitude's extensive?
- Can you readily discern numerous sources of gratitude within the tapestry of your surroundings?
- Has your appreciation for existence and human connection deepened with the passage of time?
- Do you frequently experience moments of gratitude towards specific individuals or entities?

- Do you extend your appreciation to a diverse spectrum of individuals?

Affirmative responses to many of these questions suggest a robust sense of gratitude, while negative responses warrant consideration of strategies to cultivate gratitude in your life.

Typology of Gratitude

Gratitude can be categorized tripartitely:

- Affective Trait: An inherent disposition that governs an individual's tendency to experience gratitude. While some individuals naturally possess a greater propensity for gratitude, research does not conclusively establish a correlation with established personality traits like conscientiousness, agreeableness, or extroversion.
- Mood: A transient state that can oscillate over time. Individuals may experience periods of heightened gratitude followed by periods of diminished gratitude.
- Emotion: A fleeting sensation experienced in the present moment. Gratitude can be elicited by specific encounters or experiences.

Cultivating Gratitude: A Practical Guide

The development of a profound sense of gratitude transcends complexity and arduousness. Its realization necessitates neither specialized instruments nor arduous training. Conversely, consistent practice fosters proficiency and cultivates a perpetual state of appreciation. Here is a comprehensive guide to facilitate the practice:

Momentary Observation:

Pause and introspect upon your present experience and emotions. Engage your senses and reflect on the factors that contribute to your well-being. Acknowledge the individuals who have extended their assistance or the specific circumstances that alleviate stress, enhance contentment, or facilitate your accomplishments. Mindfulness practices, which cultivate a heightened awareness of the present moment, can prove invaluable in this regard.

Gratitude Journaling:

Consider maintaining a gratitude journal where you meticulously document a handful of daily blessings. The ability to revisit these observations can provide solace during times of gratitude deficiency.

Momentary Savouring:

Indulge in the present moment and relish its essence. Focus on the experience and permit yourself to absorb the accompanying positive emotions.

Gratitude Rituals:

Incorporating pauses for appreciation and expressing gratitude can amplify your feelings of gratitude. Meditation, prayer, or mantras represent examples of rituals that foster a heightened sense of gratitude.

Gratitude Expression:

Gratitude encompasses recognizing and valuing the individuals, circumstances, moments, abilities, or gifts that enrich our lives with joy, serenity, or solace. Express your appreciation through verbal acknowledgements or silent reflection upon your blessings.

Interpersonal Impact:

Gratitude expression holds significant implications for interpersonal relationships, particularly with intimate partners. Individuals with a high capacity for gratitude experience a marked decline in marital satisfaction when their partners fail to reciprocate gratitude. Demonstrating appreciation for loved ones can enhance the quality and fulfilment of relationships.

Enhanced Well-being through the Lens of Gratitude

Gratitude fosters a profound impact on individuals' holistic well-being, as evidenced by empirical research. Its myriad benefits include:

- **Augmented Restful Sleep:** Gratitude promotes relaxation and reduces mental chatter, facilitating deeper slumber.
- **Strengthened Immune System:** Studies suggest that gratitude enhances immune function, bolstering the body's defences against illness.
- **Elevated Self-Esteem:** Expressing gratitude cultivates a positive self-image, fostering a sense of worthiness.
- **Diminished Stress:** Gratitude redirects attention to positive experiences, mitigating the detrimental effects of stress.
- **Reduced Blood Pressure:** Gratitude has been linked to lower blood pressure, contributing to cardiovascular health.
- **Alleviated Anxiety and Depression:** Gratitude suppresses negative emotions, such as worry and despair, promoting mental well-being.
- **Enriched Relationships:** Gratitude fosters connection and appreciation, strengthening bonds with others.

- **Enhanced Optimism:** Gratitude trains the mind to focus on the positive aspects of life, fostering a hopeful outlook.
- **Greater Trust:** Expressing gratitude acknowledges others' contributions, building trust and fostering a supportive environment.

Furthermore, gratitude encourages individuals to adopt health-promoting behaviours', including regular exercise, adherence to medical advice, and maintenance of a balanced lifestyle.

Psychologist Robert Emmons posits that gratitude's transformative power stems from its ability to:

- Centre individuals in the present, amplifying positive emotions.
- Foster self-worth by recognizing the support and care of others.
- Block toxic emotions like envy and regret, preserving happiness.

Inspired by an extensive literary and authorial career, I firmly advocate that the burgeoning Nigerian and African generations embrace the tenets of education, diligent effort, and pioneering innovation. By embracing these pillars, they will unlock the latent potential within themselves and make invaluable contributions to the advancement of their societies and nations.

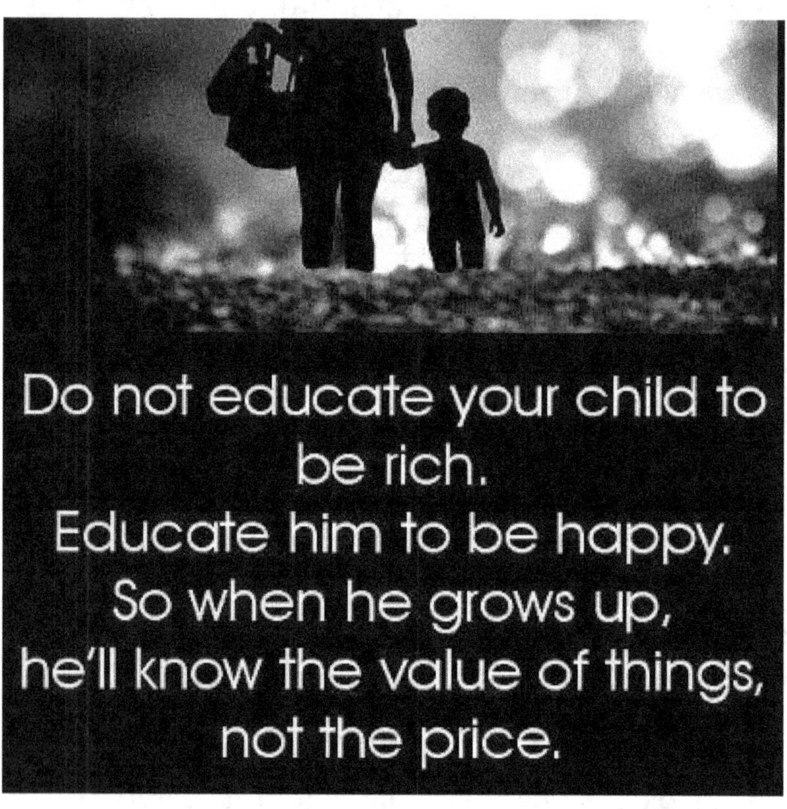

I HAVE BEEN STABBED IN THE BACK BY THOSE I
NEEDED THE MOST. I VE BEE LIED TO BY THOSE I
LOVE. AND I HAVE FELT ALONE WHEN I
COULDN'T AFFORD TO BE. BUT AT THE END OF
THE DAY, I HAD TO LEARN TO BE MY OWN BEST
FRIEND, BECAUSE THERE'S GOING TO BE DAYS
WHERE NO ONE IS GOING TO BE THERE FOR ME
BUT MYSELF.

Ha -cough- ah ha!
CHOKED ON TEA~
-cough- Ah ha!
I'll remember that sound until the day I die!
Dumbest rescue ever!
veen
Angleterre, allow me show you the proper way to tie someone up.
Je vous prie.
Slow down a minute would'ya!
Why? Does it seem too hot out to you?
Hey!!! A polarbear!
I can't help but have hope for the future...
flutter
flutter
I think I'll rest here a minute...
So many of us having fun together. Not that long ago the very idea would have been laughable.
Holyromanempire!!! Guess who's relaxing right under us!?!
Quick! Germania! Pass me another water ballon!

"WATCH YOUR THOUGHTS; THEY BECOME WORDS. WATCH YOUR WORDS; THEY BECOME ACTIONS. WATCH YOUR ACTIONS; THEY BECOME HABIT. WATCH YOUR HABITS. THEY BECOME CHARACTER. WATCH YOUR CHARACTER; IT BECOMES YOUR DESTINY."

Epilogue

The tapestry of this tale has reached its denouement, leaving but a whisper of closure and the tantalizing promise of what lies ahead.

As the curtain descends on this chapter, a portal beckons, inviting the discerning reader to venture beyond. For in the pages yet unwritten, a new odyssey awaits, fraught with unforeseen twists and turns.

Let the embers of this story flicker in your memory as you eagerly anticipate the unravelling of its next chapter.

Heavenly Father, we humbly beseech You to watch over our children with Your infinite love and protection. May Your guiding light illuminate their paths, shielding them from harm and negativity. Grant them strength and wisdom as they navigate the challenges of life, and instil in them the values of kindness, compassion, and integrity. Surround them with positive influences and nurture their spirits, so they may grow into responsible and caring individuals. We entrust their well-being into Your capable hands, confident that your watchful eye will always be upon them. Amen.